T0380567

Study Guide

Training Guide for Heaven

Running for the Prize

DAVID L. JOHNSON *and*
RICHARD A. HANSEN

WESTBOW
PRESS®
A DIVISION OF THOMAS NELSON
& ZONDERVAN

WestBow Press books may be ordered through booksellers or by contacting:

WestBow Press
A Division of Thomas Nelson & Zondervan
1663 Liberty Drive
Bloomington, IN 47403
www.westbowpress.com
844-714-3454

ISBN: 978-1-6642-2446-9 (sc)
ISBN: 978-1-6642-2445-2 (e)

Print information available on the last page.

WestBow Press rev. date: 3/26/2021

Contents

Introduction

Reading a book is fine, but we believe it is important to dwell upon and think about the topics in the book. It is important to study the topics that are vital to your future. It is vitally important, therefore, to study the Bible. Why?

We all seek answers to the following questions:

- What is my purpose in life?
- How do I do good in the world?
- Where did I come from?
- What happens to me after I die?
- How can I get to heaven?

God speaks through the Bible and answers those questions:

> All Scripture is God-breathed and is useful for teaching, rebuking, correcting and training in righteousness, (2 Timothy 3:16)

We have created this study guide to help you study our book, *Training Guide for Heaven: Running for the* Prize. The questions prompt you to think more deeply about the topics in the book. Some are easy, and some are more thought provoking.

Each chapter in the study guide identifies Key Points at a Glance, which are the main topics in each chapter of the book. For each Key Point, the study guide poses questions for thought and discussion. Therefore, this study guide is ideally used in a Bible study with other people. By listening to what other people think and what questions they have, you can seek answers in the Bible. At the end of each chapter of the study guide is a Going Deeper discussion question and a quiz with answers on a following page.

We have provided the relevant Bible verses for each discussion question in the study guide, but we encourage you to look up the verses in your own Bible. Read the adjacent verses to get a sense of the context. Read the commentary notes at the bottom. Look up related verses. Really get a sense of what the Bible verse is saying. Internalize the verse. Memorize it if it is really meaningful to you. In a sense chew on the verse to draw out all that it offers.

> Taste and see that the Lord is good; blessed is the one who takes refuge in him. (Psalm 34:8)

We hope this study guide draws you closer to God the Father, the Son, and the Holy Spirit. We hope it prepares you to go to heaven and be presented with rewards there. We also hope that it empowers you to spread the Gospel, the good news of Jesus Christ, to those who are perishing.

> Jesus answered, "I am the way and the truth and the life. No one comes to the Father except through me. (John 14:6)

1

The Most Important Question in Your Life

Key Points At a Glance:

A. Life is a journey with a beginning, middle, and end
B. You should plan with the end in mind
C. If you fail to plan, plan to fail: the importance of goals
D. Goals should be SMART

Key Points:

A

Discussion Questions:

Life is a journey with a beginning, middle, and end

1. The most important question in your life is where you go when you die. Do you agree? Why or why not?

_____

_____

_____

_____

_____

_____

2. Have you thought about dying? Does it scare you? Why or why not?

_____

_____

_____

_____

_____

_____

B

You should plan with the end in mind

1. How can this impact your purpose in life?

_____

_____

_____

_____

_____

_____

2. How does having a purpose in life make a difference in your priorities, relationships, family?

_____

_____

_____

_____

_____

3. According to the following verses, how does your belief in God impact your plans?

> Commit to the Lord whatever you do, and he will establish your plans. (Proverbs 16:3)

> In their hearts humans plan their course, but the Lord establishes their steps. (Proverbs 16:9)

_____

_____

_____

_____

_____

4. What is the goal the Apostle Paul is suggesting in the following verse?

> I press on toward the goal to win the prize for which God has called me heavenward in Christ Jesus. (Philippians 3:14)

_____

_____

_____

_____

_____

_____

5. Explain how this verse relates to making plans:

> Trust in the Lord with all your heart and lean not on your own understanding; in all your ways submit to him, and he will make your paths straight. (Proverbs 3:5-6)

_____

_____

_____

_____

_____

_____

C   If you fail to plan, plan to fail: the importance of goals
1. Provide an instance when you failed to plan and explain what were the consequences.

_____

_____

_____

_____

_____

2. Describe the process you used to plan a vacation or some other activity, such as training for a race.

_____

_____

_____

_____

_____

_____

3. Explain why it doesn't make sense to spend more time planning for a vacation than planning for your life after death.

_____

_____

_____

_____

_____

_____

4. How do these verses support the need to make plans?

> The plans of the diligent lead to profit as surely as haste leads to poverty. (Proverbs 21:5)

> Suppose one of you wants to build a tower. Won't you first sit down and estimate the cost to see if you have enough money to complete it? (Luke 14:28)

_____

_____

_____

_____

_____

_____

5. What attitude is a prerequisite for your plans to succeed according to the following verse?

> Take delight in the Lord, and he will give you the desires of your heart. (Psalm 37:4)

_____
_____
_____
_____
_____
_____

D   Goals should be SMART

1. Have you formulated goals in the past? If you have, what has been the result? What went right or wrong?

_____
_____
_____
_____
_____
_____

2. Specific: Clear and unambiguous. What are the consequences of not making your goals specific?

_____
_____
_____
_____
_____
_____

3. Measurable: Can measure your progress. What are the consequences of not making your goals measurable?

_____

_____

_____

_____

_____

_____

4. Achievable: Attainable and not impossible. What are the consequences of not making your goals achievable?

_____

_____

_____

_____

_____

_____

5. Realistic: Within reach within the time specified. What are the consequences of not making your goals realistic?

_____

_____

_____

_____

_____

_____

6. Timely: Includes a starting date and an ending date. What are the consequences of not providing a starting and ending date for your goals?

_____

_____

_____

_____

_____

_____

Going Deeper:

Use the following verse to answer the questions below:

> Do you not know that in a race all the runners run, but only one gets the prize? Run in such a way as to get the prize. Everyone who competes in the games goes into strict training. They do it to get a crown that will not last, but we do it to get a crown that will last forever. Therefore I do not run like someone running aimlessly; I do not fight like a boxer beating the air. No, I strike a blow to my body and make it my slave so that after I have preached to others, I myself will not be disqualified for the prize. (1 Corinthians 9:24-27)

1. What is the prize Paul is talking about?

_____

_____

_____

_____

_____

_____

2. What kind of crown could last forever?

_____

_____

_____

_____

_____

_____

3. What does it mean to "I strike a blow to my body and make it my slave so that after I have preached to others, I myself will not be disqualified for the prize"?

_____

_____

_____

_____

_____

Quiz

1. What is the most important question in your life?

   a. What do I want to do for a career?
   b. What happens when I die?
   c. Should I get married and start a family?
   d. How can I become a millionaire?

2. The Bible states that if you trust in the Lord and submit to Him in all your ways, He will…

   a. Eliminate the need to plan
   b. Make things happen faster
   c. Make your paths straight
   d. All of the above

3. If you fail to plan…

   a. You plan to fail
   b. You save time
   c. You save money
   d. Your life is more exciting

4. According to the Bible, planning is …

    a. Profitable
    b. Useful by counting the cost of the endeavor
    c. Not necessary; we live by faith
    d. A and B

5. What is wrong with the following goal: I will read the book of John

    a. Not specific
    b. Not achievable
    c. Not timely (no start and end date)
    d. Not measurable

6. What is wrong with the following goal: I will give more to the church

    a. Not specific
    b. Not achievable
    c. Not timely (no start or end date)
    d. Not specific, timely, or measurable

7. What is wrong with the following goal: I will start a ministry for children

    a. Not specific
    b. Not achievable
    c. Not timely (no start or end date)
    d. Not specific, timely, or measurable

8. What is wrong with the following goal: I will become a well-known evangelist.

    a. Not realistic
    b. Not achievable
    c. Not timely (no start or end date)
    d. Not realistic, achievable, timely, or measurable

Quiz Answers

1. b.
2. c.
3. a.
4. d.
5. c.
6. d.
7. d.
8. d.

2

Where Do We Go When We Die?

Key Points At a Glance:

A. Where do we go when we die?
B. What does the Bible say about heaven and hell?
C. Evidence the Bible is true
D. God's chosen people
E. Prophecies about Jesus
F. Historical accuracy of the Bible

Key Points:

A

Discussion Questions:

Where do we go when we die?

1. Is there life after death and a realm beyond the physical? Explain how you have come to your conclusion.

_____
_____
_____
_____
_____
_____

B

What does the Bible say about heaven and hell?

1. What do the following verses say about heaven (emphasis added)?

> The priests and the Levites stood to bless the people, and God heard them, for their prayer reached **heaven**, his holy dwelling place. (2 Chronicles 30:27)

> Then I said: "Lord, the God of **heaven**, the great and awesome God, who keeps his covenant of love with those who love him and keep his commandments..." (Nehemiah 1:5)

Then God's temple in **heaven** was opened, and within his temple was seen the ark of his covenant. And there came flashes of lightning, rumblings, peals of thunder, an earthquake and a severe hailstorm. (Revelation 11:19)

_____
_____
_____
_____
_____
_____

2. What do the following verses say about hell (emphasis added)?

Multitudes who sleep in the dust of the earth will awake: some to everlasting life, others to **shame and everlasting contempt**. (Daniel 12:2)

The Son of Man will send out his angels, and they will weed out of his kingdom everything that causes sin and all who do evil. They will throw them into the **blazing furnace**, where there will be weeping and gnashing of teeth. (Matthew 13:41-42)

But the cowardly, the unbelieving, the vile, the murderers, the sexually immoral, those who practice magic arts, the idolaters and all liars—they will be consigned to the **fiery lake of burning sulfur**. This is the second death. (Revelation 21:8)

_____
_____
_____
_____

C   Evidence the Bible is true

1. How does the Bible align with reality?

2. How are the Jewish people a unifying device in the Bible?

D   God's chosen people

1. What is unique about the Jewish people?

2. What does this prophecy promise to the descendants of Abraham, Isaac, and Jacob?

> On that day the Lord made a covenant with Abram and said, "To your descendants I give this land, from the Wadi of Egypt to the great river, the Euphrates—the land of the Kenites, Kenizzites, Kadmonites, Hittites, Perizzites, Rephaites, Amorites, Canaanites, Girgashites and Jebusites." (Genesis 15:18-21)

_____

_____

_____

_____

_____

_____

3. What does this prophecy predict? Has it been fulfilled?

> You who were as numerous as the stars in the sky will be left but few in number, because you did not obey the Lord your God. Just as it pleased the Lord to make you prosper and increase in number, so it will please him to ruin and destroy you. You will be uprooted from the land you are entering to possess. Then the Lord will scatter you among all nations, from one end of the earth to the other. There you will worship other gods—gods of wood and stone, which neither you nor your ancestors have known. (Deuteronomy 28:62-64)

_____

_____

_____

_____

4. What does this prophecy predict?

    "Only if these decrees vanish from my sight," declares
    the Lord, "will Israel ever cease being a nation before
    me." This is what the Lord says: "Only if the heavens
    above can be measured and the foundations of the earth
    below be searched out will I reject all the descendants of
    Israel because of all they have done," declares the Lord.
    (Jeremiah 31: 36-37)

5. What does this prophecy predict? Has it been fulfilled?

    In that day the Lord will reach out his hand a second
    time to reclaim the surviving remnant of his people from
    Assyria, from Lower Egypt, from Upper Egypt, from
    Cush, from Elam, from Babylonia, from Hamath and
    from the islands of the Mediterranean. He will raise a
    banner for the nations and gather the exiles of Israel; he
    will assemble the scattered people of Judah from the four
    quarters of the earth. (Isaiah 11:11-12)

_____

_____

E   Prophecies about Jesus

1. What was the fulfillment of the following prophecy?

> "Seventy 'sevens' are decreed for your people and your holy city to finish transgression, to put an end to sin, to atone for wickedness, to bring in everlasting righteousness, to seal up vision and prophecy and to anoint the Most Holy Place. Know and understand this: From the time the word goes out to restore and rebuild Jerusalem until the Anointed One, the ruler, comes, there will be seven 'sevens,' and sixty-two 'sevens.' It will be rebuilt with streets and a trench, but in times of trouble. (Daniel 9:24-25)

_____

_____

_____

_____

_____

_____

2. What was the fulfillment of the following prophecy?

> But you, Bethlehem Ephrathah, though you are small among the clans of Judah, out of you will come for me one who will be ruler over Israel, whose origins are from of old, from ancient times. (Micah 5:2)

_____

_____

_____

_____

_____

_____

3.   What was the fulfillment of the following prophecy?

Therefore the Lord himself will give you a sign: The virgin will conceive and give birth to a son, and will call him Immanuel. (Isaiah 7:14)

_____

_____

_____

_____

_____

_____

4.   What was the fulfillment of the following prophecy?

By oppression and judgment he was taken away. Yet who of his generation protested? For he was cut off from the land of the living; for the transgression of my people he was punished. (Isaiah 53:8)

_____

_____

_____

_____

_____

_____

5.   What was the fulfillment of the following prophecy?

He was despised and rejected by mankind, a man of suffering, and familiar with pain. Like one from whom

people hide their faces he was despised, and we held him in low esteem. (Isaiah 53:3)

_____

_____

_____

_____

_____

6. What was the fulfillment of the following prophecy?

I am poured out like water, and all my bones are out of joint. My heart has turned to wax; it has melted within me. My mouth is dried up like a potsherd, and my tongue sticks to the roof of my mouth; you lay me in the dust of death. Dogs surround me, a pack of villains encircles me; they pierce my hands and my feet. (Psalm 22:14-16)

_____

_____

_____

_____

_____

7. What was the fulfillment of the following prophecies?

But he was pierced for our transgressions, he was crushed for our iniquities; the punishment that brought us peace was on him, and by his wounds we are healed. We all, like sheep, have gone astray, each of us has turned to our own way; and the Lord has laid on him the iniquity of us all. (Isaiah 53:5-6)

Therefore I will give him a portion among the great, and he will divide the spoils with the strong, because he poured out his life unto death, and was numbered with the transgressors. For he bore the sin of many, and made intercession for the transgressors. (Isaiah 53:12)

_____

_____

_____

_____

_____

_____

8. What was the fulfillment of the following prophecy?

Because you will not abandon me to the realm of the dead, nor will you let your faithful one see decay. (Psalm 16:10)

_____

_____

_____

_____

_____

_____

F   Historical accuracy of the Bible
    1. Cite some evidence that the Bible is historically accurate.

_____

_____

_____

_____

_____

_____

Going Deeper:

1. What are the strengths and weakness about the following theories about life after death?

   a. You cease to exist.
   b. Good people go to heaven.
   c. All people who are sincere about their beliefs go to heaven.
   d. There is only one way to go to heaven, through the payment made by Jesus Christ on the Cross.

   _____
   _____
   _____
   _____
   _____
   _____

Quiz

1. What does the Bible say happens to people when they die?

   a. They cease to exist.
   b. All good people go to heaven.
   c. All people who are sincere about their beliefs go to heaven.
   d. There is only one way to go to heaven, through the payment by Jesus Christ.

2. According to the Bible, which statement is true about heaven and hell?

   a. Heaven is God's holy dwelling place, and hell is where there will be weeping and gnashing of teeth.
   b. Heaven is all around us and in us.
   c. Heaven is a state of nothingness.
   d. Hell is where there is a lot of partying going on.

3. What does the Bible prophesize about the Jewish people?

   a. They will inherit the land of Israel.
   b. They will be scattered among all the nations but God will bring them back together.
   c. Israel will always be a nation to God.
   d. All of the above

4. What does the Bible prophesize about Jesus?

   a. He will be born of a virgin in Bethlehem.
   b. He would die for the sins of the people.
   c. He would be crucified.
   d. He would be raised from the dead.
   e. All of the above

5. Which of the following is evidence the Bible is true?

   a. A great number of copies exist compared to any other ancient text.
   b. Prophecies have been fulfilled.
   c. The Bible aligns with the world as we know it.
   d. The manuscripts were written by eye witnesses soon after the events occurred.
   e. The greatest opponent of Christianity was miraculously converted into the greatest missionary.
   f. The original copies of the Bible exist for inspection.
   g. A through E.
   h. All of the above

Quiz Answers

1. d.
2. a.
3. d.
4. e.
5. g.

3

Visualizing Your Goals:
What Is It Like in Heaven?

**Key Points
At a
Glance:**

A. God's plan for the universe
B. New heaven = New earth
C. Terrain in heaven
D. What will it be like in heaven?
E. Resurrection bodies
F. Food in heaven
G. Work in heaven
H. Rest in heaven

**Key
Points:**

A

Discussion Questions:

God's plan for the universe
1. Why does the present universe need a major makeover?

> To Adam he said, "Because you listened to your wife and
> ate fruit from the tree about which I commanded you,
> 'You must not eat from it,' "Cursed is the ground because
> of you; through painful toil you will eat food from it all
> the days of your life. It will produce thorns and thistles
> for you, and you will eat the plants of the field. By the
> sweat of your brow you will eat your food until you return
> to the ground, since from it you were taken; for dust you
> are and to dust you will return." (Genesis 3: 17-19)

_____

_____

_____

_____

_____

_____

2. Will this be a renovation or rebuild?

> See, I will create new heavens and a new earth. The former things will not be remembered, nor will they come to mind. (Isaiah 65:17)

> But the day of the Lord will come like a thief. The heavens will disappear with a roar; the elements will be destroyed by fire, and the earth and everything done in it will be laid bare. (2 Peter 3:10)

_____

_____

_____

_____

_____

B   New heaven = New earth

1. Where will God reside in the new heaven and new earth?

> Then the angel showed me the river of the water of life, as clear as crystal, flowing from the throne of God and of the Lamb down the middle of the great street of the city. On each side of the river stood the tree of life, bearing twelve crops of fruit, yielding its fruit every month. And the leaves of the tree are for the healing of the nations. No longer will there be any curse. The throne of God and of the Lamb will be in the city, and his servants will serve him. (Revelation 22:1-3)

_____

_____

_____

_____

_____

_____

2. Explain how the following verses indicate that the Earth will not be destroyed but will be torn down to the foundation and rebuilt.

> But the day of the Lord will come like a thief. The heavens will disappear with a roar; the elements will be destroyed by fire, and the earth and everything done in it will be laid bare. (2 Peter 3:10)

> I will establish my covenant as an everlasting covenant between me and you and your descendants after you for the generations to come, to be your God and the God of your descendants after you. The whole land of Canaan, where you now reside as a foreigner, I will give as an everlasting possession to you and your descendants after you; and I will be their God. (Genesis 17:7-8)

> Of the greatness of his government and peace there will be no end. He will reign on David's throne and over his kingdom, establishing and upholding it with justice and righteousness from that time on and forever. The zeal of the Lord Almighty will accomplish this. (Isaiah 9:7)

_____

_____

_____

_____

_____

C   Terrain in heaven

1. What evidence is provided in the following verses that the terrain in heaven will be familiar to us?

> And he carried me away in the Spirit to a mountain great and high, and showed me the Holy City, Jerusalem, coming down out of heaven from God. (Revelation 21:10)

> The foundations of the city walls were decorated with every kind of precious stone. (Revelation 21:19)

> People who say such things show that they are looking for a country of their own. If they had been thinking of the country they had left, they would have had opportunity to return. Instead, they were longing for a better country—a heavenly one. Therefore God is not ashamed to be called their God, for he has prepared a city for them. (Hebrews 11:14-16)

_____

_____

_____

_____

_____

2. Read all of Revelation 21 and note any characteristics of the new earth you find appealing and exciting.

_____

_____

_____

_____

_____

D   What will it be like in heaven?

     1.   What do the following verses indicate it will be like in heaven?

> He will wipe every tear from their eyes. There will be no more death' or mourning or crying or pain, for the old order of things has passed away. (Revelation 21:4)

> He will swallow up death forever. The Sovereign Lord will wipe away the tears from all faces; he will remove his people's disgrace from all the earth. The Lord has spoken. (Isaiah 25:8)

     2.   Identify any pain or mourning you wish could be removed from your life.

     3.   Speculate what you think is the meaning of the "old order of things has passed away" in Revelation 21:4.

E   Resurrection bodies

1.   1 Corinthians 15:23 refers to Christ as the first fruits. What implication does that have for us?

> But Christ has indeed been raised from the dead, the first fruits of those who have fallen asleep. For since death came through a man, the resurrection of the dead comes also through a man. For as in Adam all die, so in Christ all will be made alive. But each in turn: Christ, the first fruits; then, when he comes, those who belong to him. (1 Corinthians 15:20-23)

---

2.   What are the differences between earthly and resurrection bodies that 1 Corinthians 15:40-44 discloses?

> There are also heavenly bodies and there are earthly bodies; but the splendor of the heavenly bodies is one kind, and the splendor of the earthly bodies is another. The sun has one kind of splendor, the moon another and the stars another; and star differs from star in splendor. So will it be with the resurrection of the dead. The body that is sown is perishable, it is raised imperishable; it is sown in dishonor, it is raised in glory; it is sown in weakness, it is raised in power; it is sown a natural body,

it is raised a spiritual body. If there is a natural body, there is also a spiritual body. (1 Corinthians 15:40-44)

_____

_____

_____

_____

_____

_____

3. From the following verses what do you think our resurrection bodies will be like?

> When he was at the table with them, he took bread, gave thanks, broke it and began to give it to them. Then their eyes were opened and they recognized him, and he disappeared from their sight. They asked each other, "Were not our hearts burning within us while he talked with us on the road and opened the Scriptures to us?" (Luke 24: 30-32)

> While they were still talking about this, Jesus himself stood among them and said to them, "Peace be with you." They were startled and frightened, thinking they saw a ghost. (Luke 24: 36-37)

> He [Jesus] said to them, "Why are you troubled, and why do doubts rise in your minds? Look at my hands and my feet. It is I myself! Touch me and see; a ghost does not have flesh and bones, as you see I have." When he had said this, he showed them his hands and feet. (Luke 24: 38–40)

> And while they still did not believe it because of joy and amazement, he asked them, "Do you have anything here

to eat?" They gave him a piece of broiled fish, and he took it and ate it in their presence. (Luke 24: 41 – 43)

_____

_____

_____

_____

_____

_____

F   Food in heaven

1.   What would lead you to believe that there will be food in heaven from the following verses?

> Then the angel said to me, "Write this: Blessed are those who are invited to the wedding supper of the Lamb!" And he added, "These are the true words of God." (Revelation 19:9)

> I say to you that many will come from the east and the west, and will take their places at the feast with Abraham, Isaac and Jacob in the kingdom of heaven. (Matthew 8:11)

_____

_____

_____

_____

_____

_____

2. Refer to Revelation 7:16. If there is no hunger in heaven, what do you think is the purpose of eating?

> Never again will they hunger; never again will they thirst. The sun will not beat down on them, nor any scorching heat. (Revelation 7:16)

_____

_____

_____

_____

_____

_____

G   Work in heaven
1. What types of work in heaven are implied by the following verses?

> If we endure, we will also reign with him. If we disown him, he will also disown us. (2 Timothy 2:12)

> To the one who is victorious and does my will to the end, I will give authority over the nations. (Revelation 2:26)

> No longer will there be any curse. The throne of God and of the Lamb will be in the city, and his servants will serve him. (Revelation 22:3)

> They will build houses and dwell in them; they will plant vineyards and eat their fruit. No longer will they build houses and others live in them, or plant and others eat. For as the days of a tree, so will be the days of my people; my chosen ones will long enjoy the work of their hands. (Isaiah 65:21-22)

_____

_____

_____

_____

_____

_____

H   Rest in heaven

1. Working in heaven would not be pleasurable if there are deadlines, pressure, and fatigue. Of course, deadlines are irrelevant because there is no more time; heaven is eternal. What do these verses say about rest in heaven?

> Then I heard a voice from heaven say, "Write this: Blessed are the dead who die in the Lord from now on." "Yes," says the Spirit, "they will rest from their labor, for their deeds will follow them." (Revelation 14:13)

> There remains, then, a Sabbath-rest for the people of God. (Hebrews 4:9)

_____

_____

_____

_____

_____

_____

Going Deeper:

1. Study Isaiah 65:17-25 and Revelation 21 and 22:1-4. Compare the three chapters and make a list of attractive features of heaven.

_____

_____

_____

_____

_____

_____

Quiz

1. What does the Bible say will happen to our present universe?

    a. Nothing. The universe is eternal. It always existed and will continue to exist.
    b. The earth will face another cataclysmic flood.
    c. The heavens will disappear, the elements will be destroyed by fire, and the earth will be laid bare.
    d. The Battle of Armageddon will occur.

2. What will heaven be like?

    a. We will float on clouds playing harps.
    b. Heaven will be like a new and improved earth
    c. Heaven is a state of nothingness.
    d. Heaven will be like one long church service.

3. In heaven there will be

    a. Work and rest, fulfillment and community, joy and peace
    b. Regret and pain
    c. Boring ritual
    d. No fun because there is no sin

4. We will be transformed in heaven with

    a. Resurrection bodies that will not break down
    b. The ability to arrive instantly at a destination

    c.   The ability to eat but not worry about hunger

    d.   All of the above

5. Which of the following types of work will exist in heaven?

    a.   Governing the nations

    b.   Serving God and Jesus

    c.   Building and planting

    d.   All of the above

Quiz Answers

1. c. (The Battle of Armageddon ends with the Second Coming of Jesus Christ. After He reigns on earth for 1,000 years, the present universe will be destroyed and the new heaven and new earth will be established.)

2. b.

3. a.

4. d.

5. d.

4

Are You Going to Heaven?

**Key Points
At a
Glance:**

A. A holy God
B. Does God grade on a curve?
C. How to be saved
D. Heaven or hell
E. What happens when you are saved?
F. Trinity
G. The purpose of life

**Key
Points:**

A

Discussion Questions:

A holy God

1. What is evident about God from these two verses?

> Above him were seraphim, each with six wings: With two wings they covered their faces, with two they covered their feet, and with two they were flying. And they were calling to one another: "Holy, holy, holy is the LORD Almighty; the whole earth is full of his glory." (Isaiah 6:2-3)

> Each of the four living creatures had six wings and was covered with eyes all around, even under its wings. Day and night they never stop saying: "'Holy, holy, holy is the Lord God Almighty,' who was, and is, and is to come." (Revelation 4:8)

_____
_____
_____
_____
_____
_____

2. What is the reaction of a human encountering God from these two verses?

> "Woe to me!" I cried. "I am ruined! For I am a man of unclean lips, and I live among a people of unclean lips, and my eyes have seen the King, the LORD Almighty." (Isaiah 6:5)

> Like the appearance of a rainbow in the clouds on a rainy day, so was the radiance around him. This was the appearance of the likeness of the glory of the Lord. When I saw it, I fell facedown, and I heard the voice of one speaking. (Ezekiel 1:28)

_____
_____
_____
_____
_____
_____

3. Holiness denotes separate and special. Holy is wherever God is or whatever God designates. How much leeway did God allow in building specifications when the Israelites built the Tabernacle?

> Make this tabernacle and all its furnishings exactly like the pattern I will show you. (Exodus 25:9)

_____
_____
_____
_____
_____
_____

4. How much leeway does God allow us in our daily living?

> But just as he who called you is holy, so be holy in all you do; for it is written: "Be holy, because I am holy." (1 Peter 1:15-16)

_____

_____

_____

_____

_____

_____

B   Does God grade on a curve?

1. Why is good works not a fair standard for entry into heaven? Can a "good" person go to heaven?

_____

_____

_____

_____

_____

_____

2. Can we save ourselves through good deeds?

> For it is by grace you have been saved, through faith— and this is not from yourselves, it is the gift of God— not by works, so that no one can boast. (Ephesians 2:8-9)

_____

_____

_____

_____

_____

_____

3. What is the only deed that will grant you admittance to heaven?

> Jesus answered, "I am the way and the truth and the life. No one comes to the Father except through me. (John 14:6)

_____

_____

_____

_____

_____

_____

C   How to be saved

1. Are there any holy men or women who automatically qualify for heaven? Why or why not?

> For all have sinned and fall short of the glory of God. (Romans 3:23)

_____

_____

_____

_____

_____

_____

2. Before you can be saved, you need to admit you need a Savior. The following verses instruct us to repent. How does repenting lead to the acknowledgment that you need a savior?

> Jesus answered them, "It is not the healthy who need a doctor, but the sick. I have not come to call the righteous, but sinners to repentance." (Luke 5:31-32)

> Repent, then, and turn to God, so that your sins may be wiped out, that times of refreshing may come from the Lord. (Acts 3:19)

_____

_____

_____

_____

_____

_____

3. Where have you not measured up to the holiness of God? For what do you need to repent?

_____

_____

_____

_____

_____

_____

4. Who is the only one that can save you? What does it mean to "believe in him?"

> For God so loved the world that he gave his one and only Son, that whoever believes in him shall not perish but have eternal life. (John 3:16)

_____
_____
_____
_____
_____
_____

5. Do all paths lead to heaven? If you are a sincere Buddhist, Hindu, Muslim, or Jew will you go to heaven? How does the following verse answer that?

> Jesus answered, "I am the way and the truth and the life. No one comes to the Father except through me. (John 14:6)

_____
_____
_____
_____
_____
_____

1. How can a person be saved?

> If you declare with your mouth, "Jesus is Lord," and believe in your heart that God raised him from the dead, you will be saved. For it is with your heart that you believe and are justified, and it is with your mouth that you profess your faith and are saved. (Romans 10:9-10)

_____
_____
_____
_____
_____

D   Heaven or hell

1. Who makes the decision to go to heaven or hell? By default, are people destined to heaven or hell?

_____

_____

_____

_____

_____

_____

2. To gain admission to an eternal holy heaven requires the payment by a _____ being? Fill in the blank

E   What happens when you are saved?

1. What happens when you are saved? Fill in the following blanks.

    a. _____ In him we have redemption through his blood, the forgiveness of sins, in accordance with the riches of God's grace (Ephesians 1:7).

    b. _____ Whoever believes in the Son has eternal life, but whoever rejects the Son will not see life, for God's wrath remains on them (John 3:36).

    c. _____ Consequently, you are no longer foreigners and strangers, but fellow citizens with God's people and also members of his household, (Ephesians 2:19).

    d. _____ You, however, are not in the realm of the flesh but are in the realm of the Spirit, if indeed the Spirit of God lives in you. And if anyone does not have the Spirit of Christ, they do not belong to Christ. But if Christ is in you, then even though your body is subject to death because of sin, the Spirit gives life because of righteousness. And if the Spirit of him who raised Jesus from the dead is living in you, he who raised Christ from the dead will also give life to your mortal bodies because of his Spirit who lives in you (Romans 8:9-11).

F   Trinity

1. In the following verses who is being referred to as God? Fill in the following blanks.

     a. _____ Grace and peace to you from God our Father and the Lord Jesus Christ (Philippians 1:2).

     b. _____ While we wait for the blessed hope—the appearing of the glory of our great God and Savior, Jesus Christ. (Titus 2:13).

     c. _____ Then Peter said, "Ananias, how is it that Satan has so filled your heart that you have lied to the Holy Spirit and have kept for yourself some of the money you received for the land? Didn't it belong to you before it was sold? And after it was sold, wasn't the money at your disposal? What made you think of doing such a thing? You have not lied just to human beings but to God." (Acts 5:3-4).

2. What characteristics of the Holy Spirit are mentioned in the following verses? Fill in the blanks.

     a. _____ Do you not know that your bodies are temples of the Holy Spirit, who is in you, whom you have received from God? You are not your own." (1 Corinthians 6:19).

     b. _____ But the Advocate, the Holy Spirit, whom the Father will send in my name, will teach you all things and will remind you of everything I have said to you. (John 14:26).

     c. _____ In the same way, the Spirit helps us in our weakness. We do not know what we ought to pray for, but the Spirit himself intercedes for us through wordless groans. (Romans 8:26).

     d. _____ But you will receive power when the Holy Spirit comes on you; and you will be my witnesses in Jerusalem, and in all Judea and Samaria, and to the ends of the earth. (Acts 1:8).

     e. _____ But the fruit of the Spirit is love, joy, peace, forbearance, kindness, goodness, faithfulness, gentleness and self-control. Against such things there is no law. (Galatians 5:22-23).

f. _____ And you also were included in Christ when you heard the message of truth, the gospel of your salvation. When you believed, you were marked in him with a seal, the promised Holy Spirit, who is a deposit guaranteeing our inheritance until the redemption of those who are God's possession— to the praise of his glory. (Ephesians 1:13-14).

G   The purpose of life

1. The Westminster shorter catechism states: "Man's chief end is to glorify God and to enjoy Him forever." What does that mean to you?

_____

_____

_____

_____

_____

_____

2. What did Abraham do regarding the promise of God and what was the effect? How can we do the same when we study God's promises in Chapter 8 of the book?

> Yet he [Abraham] did not waver through unbelief regarding the promise of God, but was strengthened in his faith and gave glory to God, (Romans 4:20)

_____

_____

_____

_____

_____

_____

3. In Colossians 3:2 we are to "set your minds on things above, not on earthly things." What does that mean to you?

_____

_____

_____

_____

_____

Going Deeper:

1. What Do the following verses indicate about the soul?

> Do not be afraid of those who kill the body but cannot kill the soul. Rather, be afraid of the One who can destroy both soul and body in hell. (Matthew 10:28)

> What good will it be for someone to gain the whole world, yet forfeit their soul? Or what can anyone give in exchange for their soul? (Matthew 16:26)

> Jesus replied: "Love the Lord your God with all your heart and with all your soul and with all your mind." (Matthew 22:37)

> Dear friend, I pray that you may enjoy good health and that all may go well with you, even as your soul is getting along well. (3 John 2)

> When he opened the fifth seal, I saw under the altar the souls of those who had been slain because of the word of God and the testimony they had maintained. (Revelation 6:9)

_____

_____

_____

_____

_____

_____

Quiz

1. Which attribute of God is repeated in a phrase three times to indicate its supreme prominence?

    a. Love
    b. Forgiveness
    c. Holiness
    d. Wrath

2. Likening the World Series in baseball to the Biblical plan of salvation, which of the following ways to enter the World Series is most like God's plan of salvation?

    a. You may be admitted to the World Series if you can prove you did 100 hours of community service.
    b. You pay $1,000 for a ticket to the game.
    c. You enter the stadium because anybody who shows up can go in.
    d. Your father empties his entire life savings of $1,000 to purchase a ticket for you to enter the stadium.

3. In order to go to heaven, you must…

    a. Make Jesus the ruler of your life (declare Jesus is Lord) and believe He died and rose from the dead.
    b. Spend time in purgatory until you have been cleansed of your sin.
    c. Make a pilgrimage to the Holy Land and buy indulgences.
    d. Tithe your whole life and give up sweets during Lent.

4. Which of the following statements is true?

   a. God winks at sin and will let most people into heaven if their sins are not too bad.
   b. God's standard is perfection, and He is 100% holy. Only the sacrificial payment from an infinite being for sin can buy admission to an infinite environment, heaven.
   c. All people go to heaven. God is too loving to send anyone to hell.
   d. If you don't meet the criteria of 100% holiness during your life, you can retry over and over by being reincarnated until you do.

5. Which of the following is true at the moment you are saved (accept Jesus as your Lord and Savior)?

   a. Your sins are forgiven; you are assured of entering heaven; you are admitted into God's family and viewed by God as a saint; you are indwelt by the Holy Spirit.
   b. Your sins are forgiven; but you must do penance to be forgiven for sins committed thereafter.
   c. Your sins are forgiven, but God still views you as a sinner.
   d. Your sins are forgiven, but you better watch your step, lest you forfeit your salvation.

6. What is the function of the Holy Spirit in our lives?

   a. Indwells in us, making us temples of the Holy Spirit and prompts us to live holy lives.
   b. Helps us to pray and even prays on our behalf.
   c. Equips us to lead holy lives and provides us with power to tell others about Jesus.
   d. Like a FedEx package, the Holy Spirit seals us and guarantees our arrival in heaven.
   e. All of the above

7. The purpose of life is to?

    a.   Die with the most toys
    b.   Have a building named after us
    c.   To love and be loved
    d.   To glorify God and enjoy Him forever

Quiz Answers

1. c.
2. d.
3. a.
4. b.
5. a.
6. e.
7. d.

5

Timeline for Heaven

Key Points At a Glance:

A. Saved vs. unsaved
B. Heaven
C. Hell
D. Church age
E. Rapture
F. Judgement seat of Christ
G. Tribulation
H. Second coming of Jesus
I. Millennial reign
J. Great White Throne judgement
K. Lake of Fire
L. New heaven and new earth
M. You are here

Key Points:

A

Discussion Questions:

Saved vs. unsaved

1. Without the shedding of blood, there is no forgiveness of sin. Throughout Jewish history, that has been the case. It began with the Passover in Egypt. What were the people instructed to do and why? What type of animal was to be sacrificed?

> The animals you choose must be year-old males without defect, and you may take them from the sheep or the goats. Take care of them until the fourteenth day of the month, when all the members of the community of Israel must slaughter them at twilight. Then they are to take some of the blood and put it on the sides and tops of the doorframes of the houses where they eat the lambs....

> The blood will be a sign for you on the houses where you are, and when I see the blood, I will pass over you. No

destructive plague will touch you when I strike Egypt. (Exodus 12:5-7, 13)

_____

_____

_____

_____

_____

_____

2. Once the Israelites left Egypt, they were required to observe seven festivals, one of which was the Day of Atonement. What occurred on the Day of Atonement?

> This is how Aaron is to enter the Most Holy Place: He must first bring a young bull for a sin offering and a ram for a burnt offering.... From the Israelite community he is to take two male goats for a sin offering and a ram for a burnt offering. Aaron is to offer the bull for his own sin offering to make atonement for himself and his household. Then he is to take the two goats and present them before the Lord at the entrance to the tent of meeting. He is to cast lots for the two goats—one lot for the Lord and the other for the scapegoat. Aaron shall bring the goat whose lot falls to the Lord and sacrifice it for a sin offering. But the goat chosen by lot as the scapegoat shall be presented alive before the Lord to be used for making atonement by sending it into the wilderness as a scapegoat. (Leviticus 16:3, 5-10)

_____

_____

_____

_____

3. In about 1000 BC Solomon built the Temple in Jerusalem, where the sacrifices were to take place. Jesus was crucified around 30-33 AD, and the Temple was destroyed by the Romans in 70 AD, leaving the Jewish people no place to make a sacrifice for their sins. Explain why this is not a coincidence.

> The next day John saw Jesus coming toward him and said, "Look, the Lamb of God, who takes away the sin of the world! (John 1:29)

B   Heaven

1. When a person who is saved dies today, what happens?

> Jesus answered him, "Truly I tell you, today you will be with me in paradise." (Luke 23:43)

> We are confident, I say, and would prefer to be away from the body and at home with the Lord. (2 Corinthians 5:8)

> I am torn between the two: I desire to depart and be with Christ, which is better by far; (Philippians 1:23)

---

2. What is the default condition of humans at birth?

> For all have sinned and fall short of the glory of God. (Romans 3:23)

> Whoever believes in him is not condemned, but whoever does not believe stands condemned already because they have not believed in the name of God's one and only Son. (John 3:18)

C   Hell

1. What is it like in hell (Hades) as the following account describes?

> In Hades, where he was in torment, he looked up and saw Abraham far away, with Lazarus by his side. So he called to him, "Father Abraham, have pity on me and send Lazarus to dip the tip of his finger in water and cool my tongue, because I am in agony in this fire." (Luke 16:23-24)

_____

_____

D   Church age

1.   What event ushered in the church age?

> When the day of Pentecost came, they were all together in one place. Suddenly a sound like the blowing of a violent wind came from heaven and filled the whole house where they were sitting. They saw what seemed to be tongues of fire that separated and came to rest on each of them. All of them were filled with the Holy Spirit and began to speak in other tongues as the Spirit enabled them. (Acts 2:1-4)

_____

_____

_____

_____

_____

_____

2.   What was the effect of speaking in other tongues?

> Utterly amazed, they asked: "Aren't all these who are speaking Galileans? Then how is it that each of us hears them in our native language?... (both Jews and converts to Judaism); Cretans and Arabs—we hear them declaring the wonders of God in our own tongues!" (Acts 2:7-8,11)

_____

_____

_____

_____

_____

E   Rapture

1.   What event will close the church age?

> For the Lord himself will come down from heaven, with a loud command, with the voice of the archangel and with the trumpet call of God, and the dead in Christ will rise first. After that, we who are still alive and are left will be caught up together with them in the clouds to meet the Lord in the air. And so we will be with the Lord forever. (1 Thessalonians 4:16-17)

_____

_____

_____

_____

_____

2.   How is the Rapture described in 1 Thessalonians 4:16-17 similar to Jesus' ascension to heaven described in the following verses?

> After he said this, he was taken up before their very eyes, and a cloud hid him from their sight. They were looking intently up into the sky as he was going, when suddenly two men dressed in white stood beside them. "Men of Galilee," they said, "why do you stand here looking into the sky? This same Jesus, who has been taken from you into heaven, will come back in the same way you have seen him go into heaven." (Acts 1:9-11)

_____

_____

_____

_____

F   Judgement Seat of Christ

1.   How do the following verses motivate you?

> For we must all appear before the judgment seat of Christ, so that each of us may receive what is due us for the things done while in the body, whether good or bad. (2 Corinthians 5:10)

> You, then, why do you judge your brother or sister? Or why do you treat them with contempt? For we will all stand before God's judgment seat. It is written: "'As surely as I live,' says the Lord, 'every knee will bow before me; every tongue will acknowledge God.'" So then, each of us will give an account of ourselves to God. (Romans 14:10-12)

_____

_____

_____

_____

_____

_____

2.   The Judgement Seat of Christ for believers is very different from the Great White Throne Judgement for unbelievers. What work will be rewarded for believers in the following verses? What will happen to believers whose work is burned up?

> If anyone builds on this foundation using gold, silver, costly stones, wood, hay or straw, their work will be shown for what it is, because the Day will bring it to light. It will be revealed with fire, and the fire will test

the quality of each person's work. If what has been built survives, the builder will receive a reward. [1] If it is burned up, the builder will suffer loss but yet will be saved—even though only as one escaping through the flames. (1 Corinthians 3:12-15)

_____

_____

_____

_____

_____

_____

G   Tribulation

1.   How bad is the Tribulation compared to past world wars and pestilences?

For then there will be great distress, unequaled from the beginning of the world until now—and never to be equaled again. If those days had not been cut short, no one would survive, but for the sake of the elect those days will be shortened. (Matthew 24:21-22)

At that time Michael, the great prince who protects your people, will arise. There will be a time of distress such as has not happened from the beginning of nations until then. But at that time your people—everyone whose name is found written in the book—will be delivered. (Daniel 12:1)

Wail, for the day of the Lord is near; it will come like destruction from the Almighty. Because of this, all hands will go limp, every heart will melt with fear. Terror will seize them, pain and anguish will grip them; they will writhe like a woman in labor. They will look aghast at each other, their faces aflame. (Isaiah 13:6-8)

How awful that day will be! No other will be like it. It will be a time of trouble for Jacob, but he will be saved out of it. (Jeremiah 30:7)

_____
_____
_____
_____
_____
_____

H   Second coming of Jesus

1.   The world would be entirely destroyed if not for the second coming of Jesus. When Jesus was being tried before Caiaphas, the High Priest, the night Jesus was arrested, Caiaphas asked Jesus if He was the Messiah and Son of God. Jesus answered below:

"You have said so," Jesus replied. "But I say to all of you: From now on you will see the Son of Man sitting at the right hand of the Mighty One and coming on the clouds of heaven." Then the high priest tore his clothes and said, "He has spoken blasphemy! Why do we need any more witnesses? Look, now you have heard the blasphemy." (Matthew 26:64-65)

Why does the High Priest accuse Jesus of blasphemy?

_____
_____
_____
_____
_____
_____

2. Jesus refers to Himself as the "Son of Man." This phrase is also used in Daniel 7:13-14. How does the Son of Man come? What do the peoples of every language do? How long will His kingdom last?

> In my vision at night I looked, and there before me was one like a son of man, coming with the clouds of heaven. He approached the Ancient of Days and was led into his presence. He was given authority, glory and sovereign power; all nations and peoples of every language worshiped him. His dominion is an everlasting dominion that will not pass away, and his kingdom is one that will never be destroyed. (Daniel 7:13-14)

_____

_____

_____

_____

_____

_____

3. How does the Son of Man come in the following verses?

> Then will appear the sign of the Son of Man in heaven. And then all the peoples of the earth will mourn when they see the Son of Man coming on the clouds of heaven, with power and great glory (Matthew 24:30)

> "You have said so," Jesus replied. "But I say to all of you: From now on you will see the Son of Man sitting at the right hand of the Mighty One and coming on the clouds of heaven." (Matthew 26:64)

> Look, he is coming with the clouds, and every eye will see him, even those who pierced him, and all peoples on

earth will mourn because of him. So shall it be! Amen. (Revelation 1:7)

_____

_____

_____

_____

_____

_____

I   Millennial Reign

1. How long does Jesus reign on this earth after the Tribulation?

> I saw thrones on which were seated those who had been given authority to judge. And I saw the souls of those who had been beheaded because of their testimony about Jesus and because of the word of God. They had not worshiped the beast or its image and had not received its mark on their foreheads or their hands. They came to life and reigned with Christ a thousand years. (Revelation 20:4)

> When the thousand years are over, Satan will be released from his prison (Revelation 20:7)

_____

_____

_____

_____

_____

2. What does the name of Jesus indicate?

> On his robe and on his thigh he has this name written: King of Kings and Lord of Lords. (Revelation 19:16)

_____
_____
_____
_____
_____

J   Great White Throne Judgement

1.   From the following verses, how are the dead from Hades (hell) judged?

> Then I saw a great white throne and him who was seated on it. The earth and the heavens fled from his presence, and there was no place for them. And I saw the dead, great and small, standing before the throne, and books were opened. Another book was opened, which is the book of life. The dead were judged according to what they had done as recorded in the books. The sea gave up the dead that were in it, and death and Hades gave up the dead that were in them, and each person was judged according to what they had done. [1] Then death and Hades were thrown into the lake of fire. The lake of fire is the second death. Anyone whose name was not found written in the book of life was thrown into the lake of fire. (Revelation 20:11-15)

_____
_____
_____
_____
_____

2. What good will "what they have done" (works) be in their defense?

> For it is by grace you have been saved, through faith—and this is not from yourselves, it is the gift of God—not by works, so that no one can boast. (Ephesians 2:8-9)

> Since you call on a Father who judges each person's work impartially, live out your time as foreigners here in reverent fear. For you know that it was not with perishable things such as silver or gold that you were redeemed from the empty way of life handed down to you from your ancestors, but with the precious blood of Christ, a lamb without blemish or defect. (1 Peter 1:17-19)

_____
_____
_____
_____
_____
_____

3. Who, then, will be saved?

> Nothing impure will ever enter it [heaven], nor will anyone who does what is shameful or deceitful, but only those whose names are written in the Lamb's book of life. (Revelation 21:27)

_____
_____
_____
_____
_____
_____

K   Lake of Fire

1. The destination of those whose names are not written in the Lamb's Book of Life is where?

> Then death and Hades were thrown into the lake of fire. The lake of fire is the second death. Anyone whose name was not found written in the book of life was thrown into the lake of fire. (Revelation 20:14-15)

_____

_____

_____

_____

_____

_____

2. What is the significance of the word "Lamb" in the Lamb's Book of Life? How does one's name get entered into the book?

_____

_____

_____

_____

_____

L   New heaven and new earth

1. What will happen to the old universe?

> But the day of the Lord will come like a thief. The heavens will disappear with a roar; the elements will be destroyed by fire, and the earth and everything done in it will be laid bare. Since everything will be destroyed in this way, what kind of people ought you to be? You ought to live holy and godly lives as you look forward to the day

of God and speed its coming. That day will bring about the destruction of the heavens by fire, and the elements will melt in the heat. But in keeping with his promise we are looking forward to a new heaven and a new earth, where righteousness dwells. (2 Peter 3:10-13)

_____
_____
_____
_____
_____
_____

2. What does John see in the following verse?

Then I saw a new heaven and a new earth, for the first heaven and the first earth had passed away, and there was no longer any sea. (Revelation 21:1)

_____
_____
_____
_____
_____

3. Who will be living there?

And I heard a loud voice from the throne saying, "Look! God's dwelling place is now among the people, and he will dwell with them. They will be his people, and God himself will be with them and be their God." (Revelation 21:3)

_____
_____

_____

_____

_____

_____

M   You are here

1. Of the following four indications that we are close to the end times, which is the most significant to you?

   a. Israel has been restored as a country
   b. An alliance of prophesied countries hostile to Israel has been formed.
   c. Third Temple preparations have been made.
   d. Technology for the mark of the Beast has been developed.

_____

_____

_____

_____

_____

Going Deeper:

Compare the sets of verses for the Rapture with the verse for the Second Coming and identify differences:

	Rapture	Second Coming
Does Jesus fetch people or bring others with Him?		
Is the mission to rescue or to punish?		

Is the purpose of the verses to encourage people or warn people of God's wrath?		

RAPTURE

Do not let your hearts be troubled. You believe in God; believe also in me. My Father's house has many rooms; if that were not so, would I have told you that I am going there to prepare a place for you? And if I go and prepare a place for you, I will come back and take you to be with me that you also may be where I am. (John 14:1-3)

I declare to you, brothers and sisters, that flesh and blood cannot inherit the kingdom of God, nor does the perishable inherit the imperishable. Listen, I tell you a mystery: We will not all sleep, but we will all be changed—in a flash, in the twinkling of an eye, at the last trumpet. For the trumpet will sound, the dead will be raised imperishable, and we will be changed. (1 Corinthians 15:50-52)

Brothers and sisters, we do not want you to be uninformed about those who sleep in death, so that you do not grieve like the rest of mankind, who have no hope. For we believe that Jesus died and rose again, and so we believe that God will bring with Jesus those who have fallen asleep in him. According to the Lord's word, we tell you that we who are still alive, who are left until the coming of the Lord, will certainly not precede those who have fallen asleep. For the Lord himself will come down from heaven, with a loud command, with the voice of the archangel and with the

trumpet call of God, and the dead in Christ will rise first. After that, we who are still alive and are left will be caught up together with them in the clouds to meet the Lord in the air. And so we will be with the Lord forever. Therefore encourage one another with these words. (1 Thessalonians 4:13-18)

SECOND COMING

I saw heaven standing open and there before me was a white horse, whose rider is called Faithful and True. With justice he judges and wages war. His eyes are like blazing fire, and on his head are many crowns. He has a name written on him that no one knows but he himself. He is dressed in a robe dipped in blood, and his name is the Word of God. The armies of heaven were following him, riding on white horses and dressed in fine linen, white and clean. Coming out of his mouth is a sharp sword with which to strike down the nations. "He will rule them with an iron scepter." He treads the winepress of the fury of the wrath of God Almighty. On his robe and on his thigh he has this name written: King of Kings and Lord of Lords. (Revelation 19:11-16)

Quiz

1. The Israelites sacrificed an unblemished lamb during this religious festival, and it was the day that Jesus was crucified. What is the name of this Jewish festival?

    a. Day of Atonement
    b. Passover
    c. Easter
    d. Pentecost

2. What is the default condition of humans?

    a. Sinful and destined for hell unless a Savior intervenes
    b. Good and destined for heaven unless they commit some heinous crime

  c. Sinful and destined for hell unless the person can perform sufficient good works

  d. Good and destined for heaven if they try very hard to be tolerant of other peoples' views

3. What began and will close the Church Age?

  a. Begin: Creation
    End: new heaven and new earth
  b. Begin: Receipt of Ten Commandments
    End: Jesus' crucifixion
  c. Begin: Jesus' birth
    End: Jesus' death
  d. Begin: Pentecost
    End: Rapture

4. Those who are saved (accepted Jesus as Savior and Lord) will be judged and rewarded for works built on the foundation of the Gospel at what time?

  a. Judgement Seat of Christ
  b. Great White Throne Judgement
  c. Millennial Reign
  d. Second Coming of Christ

5. Which of the following is true?

  a. Both the saved and unsaved are punished for their sins.
  b. The unsaved are evaluated on their good works; if they measure up, they are saved.
  c. Those saved will not be punished for their sins but will be rewarded for works built on the foundation of the Gospel.
  d. Those who are unsaved will be evaluated on their works, and none will qualify them for heaven. The only work that will qualify them is the death and resurrection of Jesus, and they rejected Jesus.
  e. C and D

6. The difference between Jesus coming at the Rapture and Jesus' Second Coming is

   a. Nothing. They are one and the same event.
   b. During the Rapture, Jesus does not come down to earth; He meets the saved in the air. During the Second Coming, Jesus comes to earth to save Israel and establish His millennial kingdom.
   c. During the Rapture, Jesus comes to earth to defeat Israel's enemies, returns to heaven, and at the end of 1,000 years, returns to usher in the new heaven and new earth.
   d. The Rapture is the same as the resurrection of Jesus. The Second Coming occurs after the earth is destroyed and the new heaven and earth appear.

7. The Tribulation lasts for how long?

   a. 7 years
   b. 3.5 years
   c. 7 weeks
   d. 1,000 years

8. Satan, his demons, and the unsaved are ultimately destined for?

   a. Hell
   b. Purgatory
   c. Oblivion
   d. Lake of Fire

Quiz Answers

1. b.
2. a.
3. d.
4. a.
5. e.
6. b.
7. a.
8. d.

6

Crowns and Rewards to Train for

Key Points At a Glance:

A. Motivations to earn rewards
B. Crown of righteousness
C. Crown of rejoicing
D. Crown of life
E. Crown of glory
F. Imperishable crown
G. Positions in heaven

Key Points:

A

Discussion Questions:

Motivations to earn rewards

1. What does God examine to reward people for their deeds according to the following verse?

> I the Lord search the heart and examine the mind, to reward each person according to their conduct, according to what their deeds deserve. (Jeremiah 17:10)

_____

_____

_____

_____

_____

_____

2. According to Matthew 22:34-40, what should be our motivation to earn rewards in heaven?

> Hearing that Jesus had silenced the Sadducees, the Pharisees got together. One of them, an expert in the law, tested him with this question: "Teacher, which is the greatest commandment in the Law?" Jesus replied: "Love the Lord your God with all your heart and with all your

soul and with all your mind.' This is the first and greatest commandment. And the second is like it: 'Love your neighbor as yourself.' All the Law and the Prophets hang on these two commandments." (Matthew 22:34-40)

_____

_____

_____

_____

_____

_____

B   Crown of righteousness

1. The following verse reveals the crown of righteousness. How do you earn it?

> Now there is in store for me the crown of righteousness, which the Lord, the righteous Judge, will award to me on that day—and not only to me, but also to all who have longed for his appearing. (2 Timothy 4:8)

_____

_____

_____

_____

_____

_____

2. According to the following verses, what might be the motivation to long for Jesus's appearing?

> The fear of the Lord is pure, enduring forever. The decrees of the Lord are firm, and all of them are righteous. They are more precious than gold, than much pure gold; they are sweeter than honey, than honey from the honeycomb.

By them your servant is warned; in keeping them there is great reward. (Psalm 19:9-11)

_____
_____
_____
_____
_____
_____

3. According to the following verses, what is the result of keeping God's decrees?

> All his laws are before me; I have not turned away from his decrees. I have been blameless before him and have kept myself from sin. The Lord has rewarded me according to my righteousness, according to the cleanness of my hands in his sight. (Psalm 18:22-24)

_____
_____
_____
_____
_____
_____

C   Soul-winner's crown

1. In the following verses, who is the "you" Paul is referring to that is the object of the soul-winner's crown?

> For what is our hope, our joy, or the crown in which we will glory in the presence of our Lord Jesus when he comes? Is it not you? Indeed, you are our glory and joy. (1 Thessalonians 2:19-20)

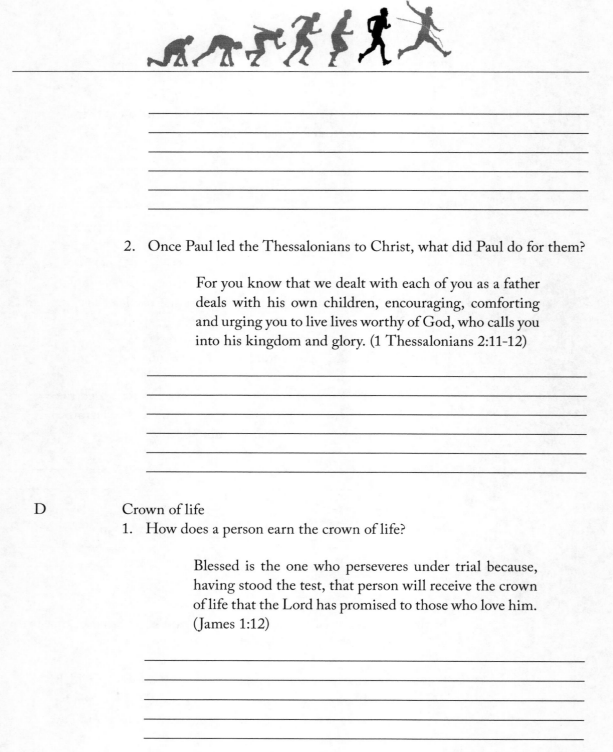

_____

_____

_____

_____

_____

_____

2. Once Paul led the Thessalonians to Christ, what did Paul do for them?

> For you know that we dealt with each of you as a father deals with his own children, encouraging, comforting and urging you to live lives worthy of God, who calls you into his kingdom and glory. (1 Thessalonians 2:11-12)

_____

_____

_____

_____

_____

_____

D   Crown of life

1. How does a person earn the crown of life?

> Blessed is the one who perseveres under trial because, having stood the test, that person will receive the crown of life that the Lord has promised to those who love him. (James 1:12)

_____

_____

_____

_____

_____

2. According to the following verses, not any persecution will earn the crown of life. What kind of persecution will earn the crown?

> Blessed are you when people insult you, persecute you and falsely say all kinds of evil against you because of me. Rejoice and be glad, because great is your reward in heaven, for in the same way they persecuted the prophets who were before you. (Matthew 5:11-12)

> Blessed are you when people hate you, when they exclude you and insult you and reject your name as evil, because of the Son of Man. Rejoice in that day and leap for joy, because great is your reward in heaven. For that is how their ancestors treated the prophets (Luke 6:22-23)

_____
_____
_____
_____
_____
_____

3. What should be our response to those who persecute us?

> You have heard that it was said, Love your neighbor and hate your enemy. But I tell you, love your enemies and pray for those who persecute you, that you may be children of your Father in heaven. He causes his sun to rise on the evil and the good, and sends rain on the righteous and the unrighteous. If you love those who love you, what reward will you get? Are not even the tax collectors doing that? And if you greet only your own people, what are you doing more than others? Do not even pagans do that? (Matthew 5:43-47)

_____
_____
_____
_____
_____
_____

E   Crown of glory

1. According to the following verses, how do you earn the crown of glory?

> Be shepherds of God's flock that is under your care, watching over them—not because you must, but because you are willing, as God wants you to be; not pursuing dishonest gain, but eager to serve; not lording it over those entrusted to you, but being examples to the flock. And when the Chief Shepherd appears, you will receive the crown of glory that will never fade away. (1 Peter 5:2-4)

_____
_____
_____
_____
_____
_____

2. In 1 Peter 5:2-4, who are "God's flock?" What are the qualities of a good shepherd?

_____
_____
_____
_____
_____
_____

F   Crown of victory

1. According to the following verses, how do you earn the crown of victory?

> Do you not know that in a race all the runners run, but only one gets the prize? Run in such a way as to get the prize. Everyone who competes in the games goes into strict training. They do it to get a crown that will not last, but we do it to get a crown that will last forever. (1 Corinthians 9:24-25)

_____

_____

_____

_____

_____

_____

2. In 1 Corinthians 9:24-25, what "way" (Run in such a way) and "strict training" will earn you the prize?

_____

_____

_____

_____

_____

_____

G   Positions in heaven

1. According to the following verses, what will be the ultimate disposition of crowns earned?

> The twenty-four elders fall down before him who sits on the throne and worship him who lives for ever and ever. They lay their crowns before the throne and say: "You are worthy, our Lord and God, to receive glory and

honor and power, for you created all things, and by your will they were created and have their being." (Revelation 4:10-11)

_____

_____

_____

_____

_____

2. If crowns are exchanged for leadership positions in heaven, what leadership positions are available?

    • _____ "Well done, my good servant!" his master replied. "Because you have been trustworthy in a very small matter, take charge of ten cities'" (Luke 19:17).

    • _____ His master replied, "Well done, good and faithful servant! You have been faithful with a few things; I will put you in charge of many things. Come and share your master's happiness!" (Matthew 25:23).

    • _____ Or do you not know that the Lord's people will judge the world? And if you are to judge the world, are you not competent to judge trivial cases? Do you not know that we will judge angels? How much more the things of this life" (1 Corinthians 6:2-3).

    • _____ And I confer on you a kingdom, just as my Father conferred one on me, so that you may eat and drink at my table in my kingdom and sit on thrones, judging the twelve tribes of Israel. (Luke 22:29-30).

Going Deeper:

1. Which of the following crowns do you think you will earn? Which would you like to earn?

- Crown of righteousness: Yearning for Jesus's return and reign.
- Soul-winner's crown: Leading others to Christ.
- Crown of life: Perseverance through persecution with love.
- Crown of glory: Modeling Christian leadership
- Crown of victory: Discipling the mind by praying and studying the Bible.

_____

_____

_____

_____

_____

_____

Quiz

1. Our motivation to earn rewards in heaven should be?

   a. To earn recognition
   b. To please God and love our neighbor
   c. To earn the biggest crown
   d. To receive the biggest mansion

2. You earn the crown of righteousness by?

   a. Becoming as self-righteous as you can
   b. Donating money for a building with your name on it
   c. Yearning for Jesus's return and reign
   d. Pointing out the sins in others

3. You earn the soul-winners crown by?

    a. Singing in the church choir
    b. Persevering through persecution
    c. Being self-disciplined
    d. Leading others to Christ

4. You earn the crown of life by?

    a. Living the good life
    b. Persevering through persecution with love
    c. Modeling Christian leadership
    d. Leading a righteous life

5. You earn the crown of glory by?

    a. Living the good life
    b. Persevering with love through persecution
    c. Modeling Christian leadership
    d. Leading a righteous life

6. You earn the crown of victory by?

    a. Discipling the mind by praying and studying the Bible
    b. Donating money for a statue that will last forever
    c. Swearing off alcohol and tobacco
    d. Persevering through tough times

7. If crowns are exchanged for leadership positions in heaven, what positions are available?

    a. Secretary General of the U.N.
    b. Ruling cities
    c. Judging angels
    d. B. and C.

Quiz Answers

1. b.
2. c.
3. d.
4. b.
5. c.
6. a.
7. d.

7

A Plan to Earn Crowns and Rewards in Heaven

Key Points At a Glance:

A. Duties not requiring spiritual gifts
B. Spiritual gifts
C. Prophecy
D. Service
E. Teaching
F. Encouragement
G. Giving
H. Leadership
I. Mercy

Key Points:

A

Discussion Questions:

Duties not requiring spiritual gifts
1. Identify some routine Christian duties that do not require special spiritual gifts.

_____

_____

_____

_____

_____

_____

B

Spiritual gifts
1. When is a spiritual gift bestowed by the Holy Spirit?

_____

_____

_____

_____

_____

_____

2. What are spiritual gifts used for?

_____

_____

_____

_____

_____

_____

3. Is a spiritual gift a natural talent?

_____

_____

_____

_____

_____

_____

4. Are spiritual gifts fully formed when bestowed?

_____

_____

_____

_____

_____

C   Prophecy
        1. What is the gift of prophecy?

_____

_____

_____

_____

_____
_____

2. Do you believe you were given the gift of prophecy? If so, why do you think that?

_____
_____
_____
_____
_____
_____

3. If you were given this gift, what is your goal to employ this spiritual gift?

_____
_____
_____
_____
_____
_____

D   Service
1. What is the gift of service?

_____
_____
_____
_____
_____
_____

2. Do you believe you were given the gift of service? If so, why do you think that?

_____

_____

_____

_____

_____

_____

3. If you were given this gift, what is your goal to employ this spiritual gift?

_____

_____

_____

_____

_____

E   Teaching
1. What is the gift of teaching?

_____

_____

_____

_____

_____

_____

2. Do you believe you were given the gift of teaching? If so, why do you think that?

_____

_____

_____

_____
_____
_____

3. If you were given this gift, what is your goal to employ this spiritual gift?

_____
_____
_____
_____
_____
_____

F   Encouragement
1. What is the gift of encouragement?

_____
_____
_____
_____
_____
_____

2. Do you believe you were given the gift of encouragement? If so, why do you think that?

_____
_____
_____
_____
_____
_____

3. If you were given this gift, what is your goal to employ this spiritual gift?

_____

_____

_____

_____

_____

_____

G   Giving
1. What is the gift of giving?

_____

_____

_____

_____

_____

_____

2. Do you believe you were given the gift of giving? If so, why do you think that?

_____

_____

_____

_____

_____

_____

3. If you were given this gift, what is your goal to employ this spiritual gift?

_____

_____

_____

_____

_____

_____

H   Leadership
        1. What is the gift of leadership?

_____

_____

_____

_____

_____

_____

        2. Do you believe you were given the gift of leadership? If so, why do you think that?

_____

_____

_____

_____

_____

_____

        3. If you were given this gift, what is your goal to employ this spiritual gift?

_____

_____

_____

_____

_____

I   Mercy

1. What is the gift of mercy?

_____

_____

_____

_____

_____

2. Do you believe you were given the gift of mercy? If so, why do you think that?

_____

_____

_____

_____

_____

_____

3. If you were given this gift, what is your goal to employ this spiritual gift?

_____

_____

_____

_____

_____

_____

Going Deeper:

1. Take the spiritual gift you believe you have been bestowed by the Holy Spirit. Formulate one overall SMART goal for how you will use this gift. Then create three steps, each accompanied with a SMART subgoal, to

get started on your path to achieving your overall goal. Pray about this and seek God's leading.

_____

_____

_____

_____

_____

_____

Quiz

1. Spiritual gifts are …

    a. Bestowed by the Holy Spirit
    b. Used to further God's Kingdom
    c. Can be the same as or different from a natural talent
    d. All of the above

2. The gift of prophecy is …

    a. Explaining what the Bible means and how to apply biblical principles to our lives
    b. Exhorting, motivating, and strengthening others to grow in their faith and reach their God-given potential
    c. Planning, organizing, supervising, and motivating a group of people to accomplish a common goal in a relationship-oriented rather than task-oriented manner
    d. Prompting by the Holy Spirit to proclaim God's word to edify, exhort, and comfort the church

3. The gift of service is

    a. Performing many different types of work—no matter how menial— to help others in ministry

b. Exhorting, motivating, and strengthening others to grow in their faith and reach their God-given potential

c. Planning, organizing, supervising, and motivating a group of people to accomplish a common goal in a relationship-oriented rather than task-oriented manner

d. Offering compassion and encouragement to people who are suffering

4. The gift of teaching is

   a. Offering compassion and encouragement to people who are suffering

   b. Explaining what the Bible means and how to apply biblical principles to our lives

   c. Prompting by the Holy Spirit to proclaim God's word to edify, exhort, and comfort the church

   d. Exhorting, motivating, and strengthening others to grow in their faith and reach their God-given potential

5. The gift of encouragement is

   a. Offering compassion and encouragement to people who are suffering

   b. Explaining what the Bible means and how to apply biblical principles to our lives

   c. Prompting by the Holy Spirit to proclaim God's word to edify, exhort, and comfort the church

   d. Exhorting, motivating, and strengthening others to grow in their faith and reach their God-given potential

6. The gift of giving is

   a. Sharing material resources generously and cheerfully with those in need

   b. Explaining what the Bible means and how to apply biblical principles to our lives

   c. Encouraging, motivating, and strengthening others to grow in their faith and reach their God-given potential

d. Planning, organizing, supervising, and motivating a group of people to accomplish a common goal in a relationship-oriented rather than task-oriented manner

7. The gift of leadership is

   a. Offering compassion and encouragement to people who are suffering
   b. Planning, organizing, supervising, and motivating a group of people to accomplish a common goal in a relationship-oriented rather than task-oriented manner
   c. Sharing material resources generously and cheerfully with those in need
   d. Explaining what the Bible means and how to apply biblical principles to our lives

8. The gift of mercy is

   a. Offering compassion and encouragement to people who are suffering
   b. Sharing material resources generously and cheerfully with those in need
   c. Explaining what the Bible means and how to apply biblical principles to our lives
   d. Exhorting, motivating, and strengthening others to grow in their faith and reach their God-given potential

Quiz Answers

1. d.
2. d.
3. a.
4. b.
5. d.
6. a.
7. b.
8. a.

8

Standing on the Promises of God

Key Points At a Glance:

A. Believers have eternal life.
B. Believers are members of a royal family.
C. Believers will live in heaven.
D. Believers will rule and judge in heaven.
E. Believers will receive rewards.
F. Unbelievers have eternal torment.
G. Unbelievers are members of a wicked family.
H. Unbelievers will live in darkness and heat.
I. Unbelievers will mourn and regret.
J. Unbelievers will receive punishment.

Key Points:

A

Discussion Questions:

Believers have eternal life.

1. Why is John 3:16 the most famous Bible verse?

> For God so loved the world that he gave his one and only Son, that whoever believes in him shall not perish but have eternal life. (John 3:16)

_____

_____

_____

_____

_____

_____

2. What comfort does the following verse provide to you or your loved ones?

> He will wipe every tear from their eyes. There will be no more death' or mourning or crying or pain, for the old order of things has passed away. (Revelation 21:4)

_____

_____

_____

_____

_____

B   Believers are members of a royal family.

1. What additional status does an heir of God have versus just being a child of God?

> So you are no longer a slave, but God's child; and since you are his child, God has made you also an heir. (Galatians 4:7)

_____

_____

_____

_____

_____

2. We are instructed to keep our eyes on heaven (Colossians 3:1-4) and store up treasure there that will not rust (Matthew 6:19-21). What is special about a believer's inheritance?

> Praise be to the God and Father of our Lord Jesus Christ! In his great mercy he has given us new birth into a living hope through the resurrection of Jesus Christ from the dead, and into an inheritance that can never perish, spoil or fade. This inheritance is kept in heaven for you. (1 Peter 1:3-4)

_____

_____

_____

_____

_____

3. According to the following verses, is it possible to lose your salvation after accepting Christ as Savior?

> And you also were included in Christ when you heard the message of truth, the gospel of your salvation. When you believed, you were marked in him with a seal, the promised Holy Spirit, who is a deposit guaranteeing our inheritance until the redemption of those who are God's possession—to the praise of his glory. (Ephesians 1:13-14)

_____

_____

_____

_____

_____

_____

4. According to the following verse, believers will live with God in heaven. What do you think that will be like?

> And I heard a loud voice from the throne saying, "Look! God's dwelling place is now among the people, and he will dwell with them. They will be his people, and God himself will be with them and be their God. (Revelation 21:3)

_____

_____

_____

_____

_____

_____

C   Believers will live in heaven.

1. What sensations do you feel when reading the following verses about heaven?

> In my Father's house are many mansions: if it were not so, I would have told you. I go to prepare a place for you. (John 14:2)

> The wall was made of jasper, and the city of pure gold, as pure as glass. (Revelation 21:18)

> There will be no more night. They will not need the light of a lamp or the light of the sun, for the Lord God will give them light. And they will reign for ever and ever. (Revelation 22:5)

_____

_____

_____

_____

_____

D   Believers will rule and judge in heaven.

1. Before the Lamb in heaven, the twenty-four elders sing a new song. What is your reaction to the prospect of being a ruler and priest serving God?

> And they sang a new song, saying: "You are worthy to take the scroll and to open its seals because you were slain, and with your blood you purchased for God persons from every tribe and language and people and nation. You have

made them to be a kingdom and priests to serve our God, and they will reign on the earth." (Revelation 5:9-10)

_____
_____
_____
_____
_____
_____

E   Believers will receive rewards.

1. According to the following verses, what can believers expect in heaven? Why?

> If anyone builds on this foundation using gold, silver, costly stones, wood, hay or straw, their work will be shown for what it is, because the Day will bring it to light. It will be revealed with fire, and the fire will test the quality of each person's work. If what has been built survives, the builder will receive a reward. (1 Corinthians 3:12-14)

> Do not store up for yourselves treasures on earth, where moths and vermin destroy, and where thieves break in and steal. But store up for yourselves treasures in heaven, where moths and vermin do not destroy, and where thieves do not break in and steal. For where your treasure is, there your heart will be also. (Matthew 6:19-21)

_____
_____
_____
_____
_____

117

F   Unbelievers have eternal torment.

1. Why do you think there will be weeping and gnashing of teeth for unbelievers in the Lake of Fire?

> Anyone whose name was not found written in the book of life was thrown into the lake of fire. (Revelation 20:15)
>
> This is how it will be at the end of the age. The angels will come and separate the wicked from the righteous and throw them into the blazing furnace, where there will be weeping and gnashing of teeth. (Matthew 13:49-50)

_____

_____

_____

_____

_____

G   Unbelievers are members of a wicked family.

1. What are the characteristics of the unbelievers consigned to the Lake of Fire? Why would the cowardly, sexually immoral, and liars be included with murderers?

> But the cowardly, the unbelieving, the vile, the murderers, the sexually immoral, those who practice magic arts, the idolaters and all liars—they will be consigned to the fiery lake of burning sulfur. This is the second death." (Revelation 21:8)

_____

_____

_____

_____

_____

_____

2. According to the following verses, what are the two conditions that distinguish those admitted to heaven and those not admitted to heaven? How can you make sure that you are among those admitted?

> Not everyone who says to me, "0Lord, Lord," will enter the kingdom of heaven, but only the one who does the will of my Father who is in heaven. Many will say to me on that day, "Lord, Lord, did we not prophesy in your name and in your name drive out demons and in your name perform many miracles?" Then I will tell them plainly, "I never knew you. Away from me, you evildoers!" (Matthew 7:21-23)

_____

_____

_____

_____

_____

_____

3. What are unbelievers missing in death? Why would that matter?

> They will be punished with everlasting destruction and shut out from the presence of the Lord and from the glory of his might (2 Thessalonians 1:9)

_____

_____

_____

_____

_____

_____

H   Unbelievers will live in darkness and heat.

    1.   What is the environment of hell like from the following verses?

> But the subjects of the kingdom will be thrown outside, into the darkness, where there will be weeping and gnashing of teeth." (Matthew 8:12)

> If your hand causes you to stumble, cut it off. It is better for you to enter life maimed than with two hands to go into hell, where the fire never goes out. (Mark 9:43)

> And if your eye causes you to stumble, pluck it out. It is better for you to enter the kingdom of God with one eye than to have two eyes and be thrown into hell, where the worms that eat them do not die, and the fire is not quenched. (Mark 9:47-48)

> For if God did not spare angels when they sinned, but sent them to hell, putting them in chains of darkness to be held for judgment; (2 Peter 2:4)

> In a similar way, Sodom and Gomorrah and the surrounding towns gave themselves up to sexual immorality and perversion. They serve as an example of those who suffer the punishment of eternal fire. (Jude 7)

_____
_____
_____
_____
_____
_____

I   Unbelievers will mourn and regret.

1. What do you think that people in hell are weeping about and so regretful they are gnashing their teeth?

> The Son of Man will send out his angels, and they will weed out of his kingdom everything that causes sin and all who do evil. They will throw them into the blazing furnace, where there will be weeping and gnashing of teeth. (Matthew 13:41-42)

_____

_____

_____

_____

_____

_____

J   Unbelievers will receive punishment.

1. Do you think the torment in hell is more physical or mental? Why?

> And the smoke of their torment will rise for ever and ever. There will be no rest day or night for those who worship the beast and its image, or for anyone who receives the mark of its name." (Revelation 14:11)

_____

_____

_____

_____

_____

_____

Going Deeper:

1. If you are going through a tough time now of heartache, pain, or discouragement, choose a Bible verse from one of the categories below, which are found in the book; write it on a note card; and tape it to your bathroom mirror or some other visible place where you live. Read the verse multiple times every day to restore your strength and your resolve to finish the race of life well.

   Promises

   - Eternal life
     o No more sorrow
     o Glorified bodies
   - Members of a royal family
     o Heirs to a fortune
     o Guaranteed inheritance
     o Guaranteed arrival
     o Living with God
   - Where believers will live in heaven
     o Mansions
     o New Jerusalem
   - What believers will do in heaven
     o Rulers and priests
   - Rewards believers will receive when they die

Quiz

1. For believers, life in heaven will eliminate what?

   a. Mourning
   b. Crying
   c. Pain
   d. All of the above

2. To belong to the family of God means …

    a. We live with God and are heirs to a fortune.
    b. We are heirs of God but can be written out of the will.
    c. God lives apart from us and keeps His distance because we are unworthy to approach Him.
    d. We may not make it to heaven because we are stuck in purgatory.

3. If you rely on Jesus's sacrifice alone to pay for your sins and are thereby admitted to heaven, you are promised…

    a. To live in heaven once you are sufficiently purified by the prayers of the living
    b. A mansion to live in, perhaps in the New Jerusalem
    c. A cloud to sit on
    d. A spot in line to enter the pearly gates if St Peter allows it

4. In heaven believers will…

    a. Float on clouds and play the harp
    b. Endlessly sing in a church choir and listen to sermons
    c. Have sex with forty virgins
    d. Be rulers and priests serving God

5. Believers will earn rewards in heaven for doing what?

    a. Contributing lots of money to the United Way
    b. Contributing money to build a new stadium at their alma mater
    c. Working to spread the Gospel and God's word during their lives
    d. Being an overall good person

6. Unbelievers that go to hell are promised

    a. Eternal life in the Lake of Fire, weeping, and gnashing of teeth
    b. Lots of drinking and partying and having fun, just like they did on earth
    c. Required to live another life through reincarnation until they reach nirvana
    d. To be released when sufficient people on earth pray and tithe for them

7. If you reject Jesus as Savior and rely on something else to earn your way into heaven, you are cast into hell along with the unbelievers who are

    a. Cowardly
    b. Murderers
    c. Sexually immoral
    d. Idolaters
    e. Liars
    f. All of the above

8. The account related by Jesus about the rich man in hell provides the warning…

    a. Your riches on earth provide no comfort in hell.
    b. There is an unbridgeable gulf between heaven and hell.
    c. There is torment in hell.
    d. All of the above

9. Hell is characterized by…

    a. Unremitting heat
    b. Darkness
    c. Separation from God
    d. All of the above

10. The response of people in hell is…

    a.   Continued sinful living, having fun, and partying
    b.   Standing proudly and shaking their fists at God in defiance
    c.   Weeping and gnashing of teeth
    d.   Drinking and carousing with sinful friends, just like they did on earth

Quiz Answers

1. d.
2. a.
3. b.
4. d.
5. c.
6. a.
7. f.
8. d.
9. d.
10. c.

Plan of Salvation

Good News

- Men and women are sinners—we are born into sin.
- God the Father cannot tolerate sin.
- But God loves you and wants you to be with Him in heaven.
- God sent His only Son, Jesus, to pay the debt for your sins.
- Only Jesus, who is God, can pay this debt.
- He died on the cross for your sins.
- He rose from the dead three days later.
- You need to repent of your sins and trust in Jesus as your Savior.

God loves you so much that He gave His only Son, Jesus Christ, to die for your sins. If you believe in Him, turn from your sins, and make Jesus the Lord of your life, you will have eternal life with Him in heaven.

Will You Pray This Prayer Today?

Dear God,

I know I'm a sinner, and I ask for your forgiveness. I believe Jesus Christ is Your Son. I believe that He died for my sin and that you raised Him to life. I want to trust Him as my Savior and follow Him as Lord, from this day forward. Guide my life and help me to do your will. I pray this in the name of Jesus. Amen.

_____   _____
            Date   Signature

If you have prayed this prayer and accepted Jesus Christ into your life by faith, please contact us at TrainingGuideMinistry.com

About the Authors

David Johnson is a former college teacher with a Ph.D. in education, has served for many years in a prison ministry, is a certified chaplain, and is a member of a large non-denominational evangelical church in the Twin Cities, Minnesota.

Richard Hansen is a retired commercial airline pilot, has served for many years in a prison ministry and a nursing home ministry, is a licensed chaplain, and is also a member of the same church in the Twin Cities.

Contact Us

By mail:

Training Guide Ministry
P.O. Box 533
Shakopee, MN 55379

Online:

TrainingGuideMinistry.com
Info@TrainingGuideMinistry.com

Printed in the United States
by Baker & Taylor Publisher Services